W9-ASN-960

THE RISE
OF
MAMMALS

The incredible
story of
life on Earth

66 million years ago
to present day

Thanks to the creative team:
Senior Editor: Alice Peebles
Designer: Lauren Woods and collaborate agency
Consultant: Paolo Viscardi

Hungry Tomato™
A division of Lerner Publishing Group, Inc.
241 First Avenue North
Minneapolis, MN 55401 USA

For reading levels and more information, look up this title at www.lernerbooks.com.

Main body text set in Burbank Big Regular Medium.
Typeface provided by House Industries.

Library of Congress Cataloging-in-Publication Data
The Cataloging-in-Publication Data for *The Rise of Mammals* is on file at the Library of Congress.
ISBN 978-1-4677-6351-6 (lib. bdg.)
ISBN 978-1-4677-7197-9 (pbk.)
ISBN 978-1-4677-7198-6 (EB pdf)

Manufactured in the United States of America
1 - VP - 7/15/15

THE RISE OF MAMMALS

By Matthew Rake

Illustrated by Pete Minister

HUNGRY TOMATO™

MINNEAPOLIS

Everything alive
today is related to
life from the past.

CONTENTS

The Rise of the Mammals   6

Evolution Timeline   8

Amazing Mammals   10
Paleogene: 56-45 mya*

Meet the Meat Eaters   12
Paleogene: 60-0 mya

A Whale of a Time   14
Paleogene: 16-2.6 mya

Monstrous Mammals   16
Paleogene: 34-5 mya

The Killer Pigs   18
Paleogene: 37-16 mya

Walking Whales   20
Paleogene: 50-0 mya

Terror Birds   22
Paleogene: 60-2 mya

Marvelous Marsupials   24
Quaternary: 1.8 mya-40,000 years ago

Monkey Business   26
Neogene: 5-0 mya

Magnificent Mammoths   28
Neogene: 5 mya-4,000 years ago

Did You Know?   30

Index   32

* mya means "million years ago"

Hi, my name is Ackerley. I'm an Acanthostega.

I'm your guide, and I've got the world's greatest story to tell you: how life evolved on Earth. Or to put it another way...

...How we all got here.

This is the fourth book in the series. In the first three, The Dawn of Planet Earth, Dinosaurs Rule, and The Last Days of the Dinosaurs, we found out how tiny organisms evolved into huge dinosaurs.

In this book, we look at the world after the dinosaurs died out. Mammals became the rulers of the world and some were every bit as frightening as the dinosaurs.

Take the rhinoceros-sized killer pigs, with skulls the size of trash cans and super-powerful jaws. Or the 49-foot (15-meter) Leviathan whale with 14-inch (36-centimeter) teeth. That's longer than your forearm and hand together.

How do we know this stuff?

Scientists who study the history of living things are known as paleontologists. To learn about life in the past, they find and study fossils. Fossils are simply the remains of animals and plants that have been preserved in rocks.

There are two types of fossil: body fossils and trace fossils. A body fossil preserves the actual parts of an animal or plant. A trace fossil preserves the marks that organisms have made. For example, an animal may have made a burrow or footprints, or a plant may have left holes where its roots once were.

It's not just mammals that were scary.

Terror birds were taller than humans and with huge pointed beaks, became the top predators in South America.

And if you think the great white shark in your world is pretty scary, you should get to know the Megalodon shark. It lived at the same time as the Leviathan whale, and you can see what happened when they went head-to-head in the most epic underwater fight ever.

So hold tight and keep reading!

Changing Shape of the Planet

You may think the map of the world has always looked the same. But the continents have changed dramatically throughout the history of Earth, just as animals and plants have.

About 225 million years ago, the whole world was one big supercontinent called Pangea.

About - 225 million years ago

Pangea

About 200 million years ago, the continent of Pangea was dividing into Laurasia in the north and Gondwanaland in the south.

About - 200 million years ago

Laurasia

Gondwanaland

By 65 million years ago, when the dinosaurs were wiped out, the world was looking much more like it does today. Laurasia was splitting up into North America in the west and Europe and Asia in the east. Gondwanaland had split into South America, Africa, India, and Antarctica/Australia.

About - 65 million years ago

In the last 65 million years, North and South America have joined up, Antarctica and Australia separated, and India merged with the continent of Asia.

EVOLUTION TIMELINE

The story begins with the Big Bang 15,000 million years ago (mya). Life on Earth starts around 3,800 mya. Oxygen forms in the atmosphere about 2,300 mya as a waste product of photosynthesizing bacteria, in what scientists call the Great Oxygenation Event. The ozone layer begins forming in Earth's atmosphere 600 mya . This will later protect Earth from the harmful rays of the sun. These events mean that animals will eventually be able to live on land.

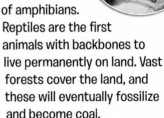

The first reptiles evolve from one branch of amphibians. Reptiles are the first animals with backbones to live permanently on land. Vast forests cover the land, and these will eventually fossilize and become coal.

Sea animals start appearing in the "Cambrian explosion of life" 540-520 mya. They swim, crawl, burrow, hunt, defend themselves, and hide away. Some creatures evolve hard parts such as shells.

Life begins on land, as plants grow by lakes, streams, and coasts, and arthropods (animals with segmented bodies, like millipedes) venture onto land. The first jawed fish appear.

Precambrian

Cambrian

Devonian

Carboniferous

Precambrian
4,540-541 mya

8

Cambrian
541-485 mya

Ordovician
485-443 mya

Silurian
443-419 mya

Devonian
419-359 mya

Carboniferous
359-299 mya

The "golden age of the dinosaurs" witnesses huge herbivore dinosaurs feeding on lush ferns and palm-like cycads. Smaller but vicious meat-eating dinosaurs hunt the great herbivores.

Homo sapiens appear in Africa around 200,000 years ago. By 40,000 years ago, *Homo sapiens* also live in Europe, southern Asia and Australia. Around 16,000 years ago, they move into North America.

Dinosaurs appear, as do the first mammals and the first flying animals with backbones, the pterosaurs.

Many different mammals evolve. Some stay on land. Some, like whales, go back into the water. Some, like monkeys, take to the trees.

Jurassic

Triassic

Quaternary

Paleogene

Cretaceous

Neogene

Permian 299-252 mya	Triassic 252-201 mya	Jurassic 201-145 mya	Cretaceous 145-66 mya	Paleogene 66-23 mya	Neogene 23-2.6 mya	Quaternary 2.6 mya - now

AMAZING MAMMALS

Mammals, like reptiles and amphibians, are tetrapods. And you know who was the first tetrapod?

Yes, that's right, you're looking at him.

You *Homo sapiens* evolved from the likes of me. Mind you, it's taken a long time for you to arrive. I grew limbs and pulled myself onto the riverbank about 365 million years ago. The first mammals came into existence about 210 million years ago, and *Homo sapiens* arose as a recognizable species about 200,000 years ago.

Mammals actually lived alongside dinosaurs for about 145 million years, but they kept a pretty low profile. Most were the size of mice and only ventured out at night. Many dinosaurs show adaptations to nocturnal hunting.

After the dinosaurs were wiped out 66 million years ago, life became less scary for mammals and they started to eat a wide range of foods and explore new places to live. Some, like primates, started to climb trees. Others, like bats and **Planetetherium**, developed wings to glide or fly. Some even returned to the water, lost their limbs, and evolved into whales and dolphins (see pages 14-15).

Stylinodon

Smilodectes

Planetetherium

These mammals all lived in North America from 56 to 45 million years ago.

Precambrian 4,540-541 mya
Cambrian 541-485 mya
Ordovician 485-443 mya
Silurian 443-419 mya
Devonian 419-359 mya
Carboniferous 359-299 mya
Permian 299-252 mya
Triassic 252-201 mya
Jurassic 201-145 mya
Cretaceous 145-66 mya
Paleogene 66-23 mya
Neogene 23-2.6 mya
Quaternary 2.6 mya - present

Humans are primates. One of the first primates was **notharctus**. It was tiny but had some features similar to those of human beings, including a relatively flat face instead of a snout, flexible hands that could grab branches, and a big brain in relation to its body size.

Did You Know?

The largest modern mammal, the blue whale, can weigh up to 210 tons (190 metric tons) and measures 90 feet, 6 inches (27.6 m). The smallest, Kitti's hog-nosed bat, is about 1.2 inches (3 cm) in length and weighs a mere 0.07 ounce (2 grams). It lives in caves in Burma and Thailand and is an endangered species. Because it's so small, it is often called the bumblebee bat.

MEET THE MEAT EATERS

The earliest dog was the **Hesperocyon**, which lived in North America 40 to 35 million years ago. It was about the size of a small fox, it may have lived in packs, either in trees or in underground burrows. The first cat, **Proailurus,** appeared in Europe and Asia about 30 to 25 million years ago.

Unlike the **Creodonts** (*right*), cats and dogs were good hunters. They were fast, powerful, and cunning, and they had excellent eyesight, hearing, and sense of smell.

Smilodon was a type of sabre-toothed cat. It roamed across North and South America as late as 10,000 years ago.

The Hesperocyon was the earliest known dog

Hesperocyon

Smilodon

Cats and dogs evolved different ways of hunting prey. Dogs and their close relatives, wolves, usually formed packs to chase their prey until it was exhausted. Big cats sometimes lived in packs as well, but they were more cunning in their hunting. They quietly crept up on their prey, then pounced.

Around 60 million years ago, some mammals started hunting other mammals. Among the first were the Creodonts. They lived from 55 to 35 million years ago and had teeth that could slice up flesh like scissors.

This made eating other animals easy!

However, they were slow, had small brains, and were not able to turn their wrists inward to trip, slash, or grab prey.

Precambrian 4,540-541 mya	
Cambrian 541-485 mya	
Ordovician 485-443 mya	
Silurian 443-419 mya	
Devonian 419-359 mya	
Carboniferous 359-299 mya	
Permian 299-252 mya	
Triassic 252-201 mya	
Jurassic 201-145 mya	
Cretaceous 145-66 mya	

Paleogene
66-23 mya

Neogene
23-2.6 mya

Quaternary
2.6 mya - present

The Creodont was one of the first meat-eating mammals.

Creodont

Smilodon had a very cunning way of killing prey. It had magnificent 12-inch-long (30 cm) canines, but its teeth broke easily and its jaws were weak, so it couldn't risk a struggle or fight.

Scientists think it pounced on its prey from the branches of trees, sank its canines into the neck of its victim, then quickly completed the kill with its powerful forelimbs.

A WHALE OF A TIME

The name of the monster shark Megalodon means "giant tooth" in Greek. Check out one of its teeth and you'll see why. It is razor sharp, serrated, and 7 inches (18 cm) long. Compare that to the teeth of the great white shark of your time: a tiny 1.2 inches (3 cm) long.

But it wasn't just the size of its teeth that made Megalodon so fearsome. It was the force with which it used them. In 2012, scientists estimated that the force of its bite was more than three times greater than *T. rex*'s bite and almost fifty times greater than a lion's.

Leviathan

Megalodon lived from about 16 million years ago to about 2.6 million years ago. Since it was the size of a bus, it needed some sizeable dinners. The giant turtle Stupendemys might have made a tasty starter. Its shell measured about 10 feet (3 m) by 7 feet (2 m), but for Megalodon it would've been like crunching on a potato chip.

For the main course, Megalodon would surely have been looking for a nice fat whale. We know it attacked whales, because bite marks have been found in many whale fossils, especially in their flipper bones and the vertebrae in the tail fin.

Megalodon

Megalodon might even have targeted **Leviathan**, a giant sperm whale that lived about 12-13 million years ago. That would be a risky move, though. Leviathan was almost as big as Megalodon and had even bigger teeth, at 14 inches (36 cm). This fight is going to be a gore fest!

MEGALODON
Location: Oceans worldwide
Length: About 52 feet (16 m)

| Precambrian 4,540-541 mya |
| Cambrian 541-485 mya |
| Ordovician 485-443 mya |
| Silurian 443-419 mya |
| Devonian 419-359 mya |
| Carboniferous 359-299 mya |
| Permian 299-252 mya |
| Triassic 252-201 mya |
| Jurassic 201-145 mya |
| Cretaceous 145-66 mya |
| Paleogene 66-23 mya |
| **Neogene 23-2.6 mya** |
| Quaternary 2.6 mya - present |

Megalodon teeth have been found in oceans all around the world, so keep your eyes open when you are by the seaside. Some vertebrae (the bones that make up the spine) have also been found. Scientists have to estimate the size of Megalodon from teeth and vertebrae, since the rest of this shark's skeleton is made up of soft cartilage, which doesn't fossilize well.

Did You Know?

Scientists think Megalodon might have first targeted the fins of a whale to immobilize it before they started feeding on the body.

15

MONSTROUS MAMMALS

If you think elephants, gorillas, and rhinos are big, how about these **super-sized** mammals that once roamed the planet...

16 f

13 f

Chalicotherium lived 25 to about 5 million years ago. The horse is probably the closest modern relative of this 10-foot (3 m) monster, but this Chalicotherium certainly didn't look like many modern steeds. Its front legs were much longer than its hind ones, and instead of hooves it had claws, which it probably used to gather vegetation. Some scientists think that it brushed the knuckles of its front feet along the ground when it walked, like a modern gorilla.

9 f

6 f

3 f

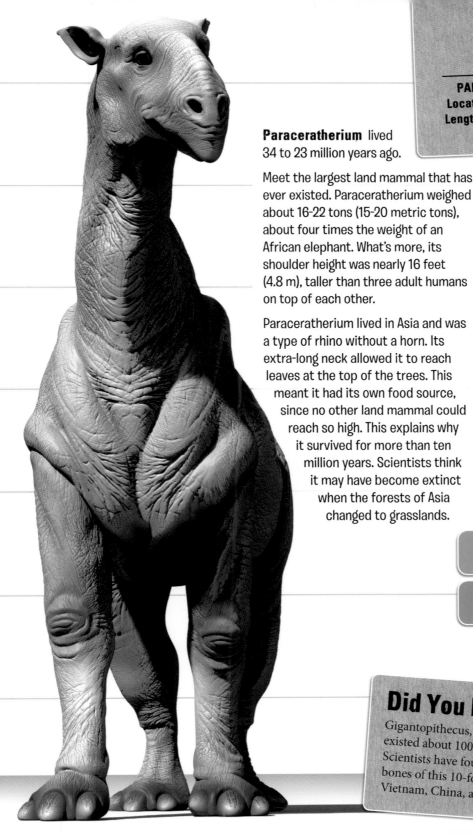

Paraceratherium lived 34 to 23 million years ago.

Meet the largest land mammal that has ever existed. Paraceratherium weighed about 16-22 tons (15-20 metric tons), about four times the weight of an African elephant. What's more, its shoulder height was nearly 16 feet (4.8 m), taller than three adult humans on top of each other.

Paraceratherium lived in Asia and was a type of rhino without a horn. Its extra-long neck allowed it to reach leaves at the top of the trees. This meant it had its own food source, since no other land mammal could reach so high. This explains why it survived for more than ten million years. Scientists think it may have become extinct when the forests of Asia changed to grasslands.

Precambrian
4,540-541 mya

Cambrian
541-485 mya

Ordovician
485-443 mya

Silurian
443-419 mya

Devonian
419-359 mya

Carboniferous
359-299 mya

Permian
299-252 mya

Triassic
252-201 mya

Jurassic
201-145 mya

Cretaceous
145-66 mya

Paleogene
66-23 mya

Neogene
23-2.6 mya

Quaternary
2.6 mya - present

Did You Know?

Gigantopithecus, a real Bigfoot, existed about 100,000 years ago. Scientists have found teeth and jaw bones of this 10-foot (3 m) ape in Vietnam, China, and Nepal.

THE KILLER PIGS

Entelodonts are often called killer pigs. And you can see why. Their jaws and muscles were specially designed for bone crushing. The bones of primitive rhinos, camels, and cows have all been found with wounds made by entelodonts. However, scientists can't agree whether these hideous hogs scavenged on dead carcasses like vultures, or attacked and killed animals as lions do.

They certainly attacked their own kind. Many entelodont skulls have been found, with gashes up to ¾ inch (2 cm) deep, which can only have been inflicted by other killer pigs. In fact, in a fight, it seems to have been quite common for one pig to fit another's head entirely in its mouth! Luckily, like modern warthogs, entelodonts had bony lumps on their skulls protecting their eyes and nose.

Entelodont

Daeodon was one of the largest entelodonts. It lived about twenty million years ago and had a huge skull about 3 feet (90 cm) long. That's about the size of a trash can! What's more, the skull had two extra-wide cheekbones adapted for its really powerful biting muscles.

Pigs are pretty harmless creatures, happy to spend their days wallowing in mud and rooting around the ground for food. Right?

Well, let me introduce you to the entelodont.

This was no ordinary farmyard pig. The smallest ones were about twice the size of today's pigs. And the biggest? They were the size of a rhino. And while the entelodonts may have been from the same family of mammals as deer, horses, cattle, and giraffes, they were certainly no peace-loving vegetarians...

ENTELODONT
Location: Asia, Europe, America
Length: Up to 11 feet (3.5 m)

Precambrian	4,540-541 mya
Cambrian	541-485 mya
Ordovician	485-443 mya
Silurian	443-419 mya
Devonian	419-359 mya
Carboniferous	359-299 mya
Permian	299-252 mya
Triassic	252-201 mya
Jurassic	201-145 mya
Cretaceous	145-66 mya
Paleogene	66-23 mya
Neogene	23-2.6 mya
Quaternary	2.6 mya - present

Did You Know?

Like modern-day pigs, entelodonts were probably omnivores, eating both meat and plants. They probably dug up roots and tubers if no meat was available.

19

WALKING WHALES

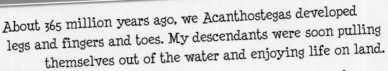

About 365 million years ago, we Acanthostegas developed legs and fingers and toes. My descendants were soon pulling themselves out of the water and enjoying life on land.

However, some 315 million years later, mammals, built for life on solid ground, started to evolve back into sea creatures, such as whales.

Why did they do this?

Probably because food was scarce on land and the sea was full of irresistibly tasty treats.

Whales didn't just lose their limbs and develop a streamlined shape ideal for swimming. Their bodies evolved in lots of other ways. Check out a few of the major changes.

Blowhole: The "nose" moved from the face to the top of the head. This meant the whale could breathe while its body was underwater.

Lungs: Whales are really good at breathing! In one breath, your body might absorb 15 percent of the oxygen you inhale. But whales take in up to 90 percent.

Blubber: The depths of the oceans are very cold, because sunlight rarely reaches below 656 feet (200 m). To keep warm, whales developed a layer of fat called blubber just below the skin.

Wolf-like **Pakicetus** is the earliest known ancestor of the whale. It was a meat eater but also liked fish, so it started evolving features to help it swim after sea creatures.

Ambulocetus, like modern whales, did not have external ears but picked up vibrations through its jawbone. To detect prey on land, it may have lowered its head to the ground and felt for vibrations.

Pakicetus lived 50 million years ago

Ambulocetus lived 50-48 million years ago

Kutchicetus lived 46-43 million years ago. Its long tail helped it move quickly through the water.

Rodhocetus lived 48-41 million years ago. As with whales, its hip bones were not fused to its backbone. This made swimming easier.

Dorudon lived 40-30 million years ago. Its nostrils, or blowhole, were on the top of its head, and its front legs were paddle-like flippers.

About 30 million years ago, whales divided into two orders:

Toothed whales, or **odontocetes**, hunt other large sea creatures. To detect prey, they developed echolocation: sending out sound pulses from their foreheads and then sensing the echo of these sounds through their jaws. The toothed whales include all species of dolphins and porpoises.

Baleen whales, or **mysticetes**, feed on small creatures and have baleen plates rather than teeth. Baleen allows them to open their mouths and take in huge quantities of small sea creatures such as krill.

AMBULOCETUS
Location: Shores of central Asia
Length: About 10 feet (3 m)

Precambrian 4,540-541 mya
Cambrian 541-485 mya
Ordovician 485-443 mya
Silurian 443-419 mya
Devonian 419-359 mya
Carboniferous 359-299 mya
Permian 299-252 mya
Triassic 252-201 mya
Jurassic 201-145 mya
Cretaceous 145-66 mya

Paleogene 66-23 mya

Neogene 23-2.6 mya

Quaternary 2.6 mya - present

Did You Know?

The blue whale, the heaviest animal ever known, is a baleen whale.

TERROR BIRDS

Can you imagine birds much taller than an adult human, with skulls more than 2 feet (70 cm) long, attached to powerful, hook-tipped beaks? Terror birds were the top predators in South America from the time of the dinosaurs to 2 million years ago.

Terror Birds

These birds didn't fly. They ruled the land. They were built like smaller versions of *T. rex*, with enormous heads, small arms, long powerful legs, and fearsome talons. Officially they are called Phorusrhacids, but that was way too hard to pronounce, so people call them **terror birds!**

There were many different species of terror birds, but most probably used the hooked tips of their large, heavy, pointed beaks to strike at prey.

Scientists think **Andalgalornis**, a type of terror bird that lived about 25 million years ago, would have wielded its beak like a hatchet, inflicting deep wounds with quick stabbing motions. Then it would withdraw to a safe distance as its victim bled to death. Grappling with the prey in a fight might have been the end for the Andalgalornis because its skull was weak.

TERROR BIRDS
Location: South America
Length: Up to 8.2 feet (2.5 m)

Precambrian 4,540-541 mya
Cambrian 541-485 mya
Ordovician 485-443 mya
Silurian 443-419 mya
Devonian 419-359 mya
Carboniferous 359-299 mya
Permian 299-252 mya
Triassic 252-201 mya
Jurassic 201-145 mya
Cretaceous 145-66 mya

Paleogene 66-23 mya

Neogene 23-2.6 mya

Quaternary 2.6 mya - present

Terror birds lived in South America before it joined up with North America. The birds ate grazing animals. Most scientists believe the terror birds were extremely nimble, swift predators that could reach speeds of 30 mph (48 kmh).

Did You Know?
Some birds might have shaken smaller prey in their beaks and even thrown their victims against the ground. This would not only kill the prey but also break their bones, making them easier to swallow!

MARVELOUS MARSUPIALS

This **Diprotodon** might be the same shape and size as a rhino, but she's a real gentle giant. She's a marsupial, in the same family as kangaroos, koala bears, and wombats. And like all female marsupials, she has a pouch in which her babies grow. This faces backward just like in modern-day wombats. In fact, diprotodon is sometimes known as the **"giant wombat."**

In modern times, there are about 235 species of marsupial in Australia and nearby islands, plus about 100 species of American marsupials.

The only modern monotreme (egg-laying) mammals are the platypus and four species of spiny anteater, all of which live in Australia and New Guinea.

Most modern mammals are placental mammals (which give birth to live young), including, of course, humans.

Diprotodon

The first mammals appeared about 210 million years ago and gave birth by laying eggs. They are known as monotremes. However, about 125 million years ago, two new types of mammals evolved: marsupials and placentals.

DIPROTODON
Location: Australia
Length: 10 feet (3 m)

| Precambrian 4,540-541mya |
| Cambrian 541-485 mya |
| Ordovician 485-443 mya |
| Silurian 443-419 mya |
| Devonian 419-359 mya |
| Carboniferous 359-299 mya |
| Permian 299-252 mya |
| Triassic 252-201 mya |
| Jurassic 201-145 mya |
| Cretaceous 145-66 mya |
| Paleogene 66-23 mya |
| Neogene 23-2.6 mya |
| **Quaternary 2.6 mya – present** |

Female placental mammals carry their babies inside their bodies until they are large enough to survive outside. Female marsupial mammals, on the other hand, give birth early to tiny babies who crawl to the mother's pouch. Here, they suckle milk from their mother until they are fully developed and ready to explore the world.

Marsupial mammals flourished in Australia where they had no competition from placental mammals. Diprotodon was the biggest marsupial to walk the earth and had no natural predators until humans arrived about 46,000 years ago. They probably hunted this gentle beast to extinction.

Did You Know?

Marsupial mammals get their name from the marsupium, the mother's pouch. Placental mammals get their name from the placenta. This is an organ inside the mother's womb that allows babies to get food from her bloodstream.

25

MONKEY BUSINESS

Around five million years ago, **Ardipithecus** and **Australopithecus** did a remarkable thing: they started to walk upright. They still climbed trees with the help of their long arms and long, curved fingers and toes. But when on the ground, they used two feet, not four.

Why did they do this?

Scientists think it was simply to save energy, raise the eyes to see farther, and free up the front limbs to carry tools and food.

Australopithecus female

Australopithecus adapted to their changing environment and about 2 million years ago they were replaced by *Homo erectus,* their descendents. These new apes had human-like proportions, with longer legs and shorter arms. They lived life entirely on the ground, made stone walls, and learned how to use fire for cooking food, hardening wooden spears, and shaping stones.

Homo erectus was one of many *Homo* species. They have all died out except one: *Homo sapiens,* better known as humans. We are one of seven existing species in the hominid, or great ape, family. The other species are two species of chimpanzee, two species of gorilla, and two species of orangutan.

AUSTRALOPITHECUS
Location: Africa
Height: 4 feet 11 inches (151 cm)

Australopithecus male

Precambrian 4,540-541 mya
Cambrian 541-485 mya
Ordovician 485-443 mya
Silurian 443-419 mya
Devonian 419-359 mya
Carboniferous 359-299 mya
Permian 299-252 mya
Triassic 252-201 mya
Jurassic 201-145 mya
Cretaceous 145-66 mya
Paleogene 66-23 mya

Neogene
23-2.6 mya

Quaternary
2.6 mya - present

Modern *Homo sapiens* evolved in Africa from about 200,000 to 150,000 years ago. But it was only 70,000 years ago that *Homo sapiens* started to travel across the world: first into Asia, and then, after a bit of island hopping, to Australia. Humans started entering Europe about 35,000 years ago and moved into the Americas about 15,000 years ago. They only reached New Zealand about 1,500 years ago, long after the Roman Empire had fallen.

MAGNIFICENT MAMMOTHS

When humans entered Europe about **35,000 years ago** in the middle of the last Ice Age, they lived side by side with woolly mammoths. We know humans hunted these members of the elephant family because several mammoth bones have been found with spear wounds.

Humans didn't hunt the woolly mammoth just for the meat. After the feasting was over, they used the pelts for clothing and the bones for constructing homes. Large bones were used as foundations, the tusks for entrances, and leg bones for the walls. Skins were probably stretched over the top to keep the rain out. Any bones left over would have been turned into small sculptures, weapons, or fuel for fires. Archaeologists discovered that 149 mammoths had been used to build one settlement at Mezhirich in Ukraine.

Woolly mammoths died out on mainland Europe, Asia, and North America about 10,000 years ago. Amazingly, though, some woolly mammoths survived on islands: on Saint Paul Island, Alaska, until 6,400 years ago, and on Wrangel Island in the Arctic Ocean until 4,000 years ago.

So how did humans kill these huge creatures? Spears were certainly used. Many dog and wolf bones have been found with mammoth bones, so some experts think humans may have also used semi-domesticated dogs and wolves to surround a mammoth and hold it in place with their growling. Maybe humans caught mammoths in pitfall traps, too. There are cave paintings that seem to show this.

WOOLLY MAMMOTH
Location: Plains of North America and Eurasia
Length: About 13 feet (4 m)

Precambrian
4,540-541 mya

Cambrian
541-485 mya

Ordovician
485-443 mya

Silurian
443-419 mya

Devonian
419-359 mya

Carboniferous
359-299 mya

Permian
299-252 mya

Triassic
252-201 mya

Jurassic
201-145 mya

Cretaceous
145-66 mya

Paleogene
66-23 mya

Neogene
23-2.6 mya

Quaternary
2.6 mya - present

Did You Know?

Human hunting wasn't the only reason woolly mammoths died out. The end of the Ice Age about 10,000 years ago probably meant the plants the mammoths ate stopped growing.

Smilodon
Pronounced: smy-loh-don

Smilodon is Greek for "saber-tooth." It wasn't big enough to prey on an adult woolly mammoth (see previous page), but it would have probably tried to pick off the young mammoths. Both these species became extinct at the end of the last Ice Age.

Megalodon
Pronounced: meg-ah-low-don

For centuries, Megalodon teeth were called tongue stones. But in 1667, Nicholas Steno, a physician to the Duke of Florence, compared tongue stones to modern shark teeth and argued that they were the teeth of extinct sharks. As a result of this discovery, many people call Steno the world's first paleontologist.

Phorusrhacids (or terror birds)
Pronounced: for-rus-rah-kids

North and South America joined up about three million years ago, and at least one type of terror bird, Titanis, migrated to North America. Its remains have been found in Florida. It was 8 feet 2 inches (2.5 m) tall, weighed approximately 330 pounds (150 kg) ,and had clawed feet that were probably used to kill its prey.

Leviathan
Pronounced: leh-vie-ah-than

The Leviathan was discovered in 2008, when a tooth-studded skull, 10 feet (3 m) long, was found in Peru. Scientists called it Leviathan after a giant monster of the Bible. However, some scientists now call it by the Hebrew name Livyatan, since the name Leviathan had already been used for a species of mastodon, a group of extinct mammals related to elephants.

Pakicetus
Pronounced: pack-ih-see-tuss

Scientists know that Pakicetus is an ancestor of the modern whale because it had an ear bone similar to what whales have, plus an ankle bone similar to the ankle bones of hoofed land mammals.

Ambulocetus
Pronounced: am-boo-low-see-tuss

Ambulocetus actually means "walking whale." This creature probably swam like modern whales, arching its spine and pushing its tail up and down in the water.

Woolly mammoth

In May 2013, an adult female mammoth, nicknamed Buttercup, was found in a chunk of ice in Siberia. She was 40,000 years old, but she was still so well preserved that even her blood was found in muscle tissue. In true *Jurassic Park* style, scientists think they may be able to clone a new mammoth from the DNA in the blood.

Diprotodon
Pronounced: die-pro-toe-don

Marsupial mammals originated in South America. About 55 million years ago, they traveled to Australia via Antarctica. (Back then all three continents were linked.) When marsupials are first born, their eyes, ears, and rear limbs hardly exist. However, their front limbs, nostrils, and mouths are well developed. This allows them to crawl to their mother's pouch and drink their mother's milk so they can keep growing.

INDEX

ambulocetus, 20-21, 31
andalgalornis, 23
australopithecus, 26-27

blue whale, 11, 21

cats, 12-13

Chalicotherium, 16
continents, 7
creodonts, 12-13

daeodon, 19
dinosaurs, 9, 10
diprotodon, 24-25, 31
dogs, 12, 29
dorudon, 21

entelodonts, 18-19
evolution timeline, 8-9

fossils, 6, 15

great apes, 26-27

hesperocyon, 12
homo erectus, 27
homo sapiens, 9, 10, 27

Kitti's hog-nosed bat, 11
kutchicetus, 21

Leviathan, 6, 7, 15, 30

marsupial mammals, 24-25,
31
megalodon, 7, 14-15, 30
monotreme mammals,
24-25
mysticetes, 21

notharctus, 11

odontocetes, 21

pakicetus, 11, 20, 21, 31

paraceratherium, 17
phorusrhacids, 22-23, 30
pigs, 6, 18-19
placental mammals, 24, 25
planetetherium, 10-11

rodhocetus, 21

sharks, 14-15, 30
smilodectes, 11
smilodon, 12, 13, 30

terror birds, 7, 22-23, 30

whales, 11, 14-15, 20-21,
30, 31
woolly mammoth, 28-29,
30, 31

THE AUTHOR

Matthew Rake lives in London, England, and has worked in publishing for more than twenty years. He has written on a wide variety of topics, including science, sports, and the arts.

THE ARTIST

Peter Minister started out as a special-effects sculptor and had a successful and exciting career producing sculptures and props for museums, theme parks, TV, and film. He now works in computer-generated imagery (CGI), which allows him to express himself with a big ball of digital clay in a more creative way than any "real" clay. His CGI dinosaurs and other animals have appeared in numerous books worldwide.